ALLOY

POEMS BY JAN BOTTIGLIERI

Jan Bottiglieri

To Haley:

Keep writing!
Best wishes for
a flowering
future —

4.22.18

— Jan

ALLOY
Poems by Jan Bottiglieri

MAYAPPLE PRESS 2015

Published by   Mayapple Press
                362 Chestnut Hill Road
                Woodstock, NY 12498
                mayapplepress.com

ISBN 978-1-936419-52-4

Library of Congress Control Number 2015902730

Acknowledgements:

Poems in this collection were previously published in:

After Hours, Aperçus Quarterly, Atticus Review, The Boiler Journal, Borderlands: Texas Poetry Review, Broad River Review, Caesura, Cider Press Review, Cloudbank, Court Green, december, DIAGRAM, Harpur Palate, Northwest Cultural Council Anthology, Prime Number Review, Rattle, Rhino, Room, Solace in So Many Words, Sugar House Review, Sugar Mule, Willow Springs.

Special thanks to the following people for their encouragement and support: poets Chris Green, Larry Janowski, and Tony Trigilio; my crash of Rhinos; my Pacific mentors and Velcros; Judith Kerman and everyone at Mayapple Press; and of course and always to John and Jake.

Cover art: "Present" by andrea bird, encaustic collage, 2010; visit *andreabird.com.* Photo of author by Jake Bottiglieri. Book and cover designed and typeset by Judith Kerman in Bell MT; cover and section titles in Castellar.

TABLE OF CONTENTS

THE PEAR

MARLENA WAS A MERMAID

MIGRATORY

THE EYE

THE PEAR

Back in the Day

When I smiled, it meant I was happy.
Everything arranged on the bone
china platter of my face
was there for ballast.

I mean balance. I could be
as composed as a salad or
as tossed, all torn edges.
When I cried,

real tears came from the corners
of my eyes. My lungs sighed like trees
and pink doors blew open and shut
in my four-room hut.

Or heart. What I said to my mirror:
In the year 2000, you'll be 36. You'll be 50
in 2013. *Que sera!* The mirror said black,
answering back. Maybe that

was more of a question.
Maybe "happy" is the wrong word.

Handkerchief

My grandmother taught me to iron
by practicing on the blank
page of my father's handkerchiefs.

Each one was flat and white as a ceiling.

I perched on the stool beside her,
just six, knowing my father
would fold square my effort, all day

I would peek from his breast pocket.

The iron: so heavy that I used
one hand to move the iron, the other
to prop my arm. The stool wobbled.

Hair stuck to my cheek, one damp curl.

Who would teach a girl to push
such a heavy, scorching thing?
Who can feel wings beat, sing

the white song trilling from my throat?

Pre-Portrait

Like birds we turned our necks
toward the black-eyed camera.
Someone pitched a best version of us

and we committed. Affixed
ourselves, a ceremony
of twist and primp and lacquer.

There was laughter, our glossy teeth
sparking like hammers, jostling, uncertain.
The room pitched, rustling the curtain.

We set eyes on that infinite
aperture, future: found
this portrait there, fixed like furniture.

We committed to memory:
the camera laughed
back its birdie. The future

came on like medication,
twisted, fixed back on that eye
and its certainty. We froze

just in time:
Now the flash
hammer swings down—

Oliver

Seven when I saw *Oliver!* on TV. I so loved that.
Soon I would be half an orphan too, but I didn't know that.

My cheek on the rug. I knew that we had everything then.
In my world, even unloved orphans sang. The movie showed that.

Raggy orphans, singing, trudged before a placard: God is Love.
At once, my doveheart beat with things it never knew before that.

What God *is*. I was less and more orphan, knowing. That proved it.
Suddenly, not just mine, love: all. A shock, almost a blow, that.

I saw too a second way the world is: true and false, at once.
Orphans singing. God and hunger. Love, and what is below that.

Seven, loved, I watched. A musical show about orphans—strange!
Still, I can think of two. Love, what can be the reason for that?

Alphabet

A is for anger, its iodine smear.
B is better than that.
C is coughing from the wings.
D is a mild disturbance, but
E shuts everyone up with its shrieking.
F is fine, thank you,
G no really, I'm fine.
H has heavy hemisphere halves:
I see them tipping their icy caps.
J-K-L and hide. That's my joke.

M makes mountains with ferocious peaks,
N nestles down between them.
O if only I could too, oblique to the
Page, Quiet, Resting on the
Slopes with the sheep and goats.
T is for tenor—no, bariTone.
U pities V for its graceless point.
WaX runs ruby off the table edge:
Y? You tell me. Maybe gravity.
Z is the arrow you can't quite see.

Summer 1972

After the twist
comes the taproot,
comes my father teaching me
to shake off the earth.

Then the fact:
and everything changed.
Everything weighed,
the handle, the heft.

After the boy
found the hammer,
he buried the claw
in the trunk of the tree.

From the branches I watched
not everyone be like me—
a switch—and with every
switch, a scare. From leaves,

I saw the claw buried.
I felt the tree tremble.
Frightened, I tried to tell: no one
seemed to think it mattered.

After the scar, the jar
of black pitch. My mother
smooths my hair.
How could I tell

what mattered? My father
was gone—this was just after.
My fingers could trace
the tree's black scar.

After the leaving.
After the leaving.
My father shaking off the earth.
I am shaking off the earth.

The Worst Gift I Ever Got Was a Grave

They say it's the thought
that counts, but with graves
I say it's the sides.
With stones, it's what's written.

It lies on a piney bump. My grave! Still
in the spot I left it. I was eight,
soft as a bag of kittens.
My mother holds the deed.

Everything that happens underground
is serious: so goes the story
of the water main and willow.
I've seen panic at the anthill,

the dug-up babies like pearly lumps.
If that was me, I'd want thousands, too.
I'd try to save them all
in my tender black jaws.

Dear grave, you have not got
mourners, a maw, me yet.
Most gifts I can't wait to open
but not this.

Not really a plan—it's more of a plot,
what you never think of at all
until you do: the lost mitten
found in spring mud. Its little wave.

'A way of happening, a mouth'

—from W.H. Auden's "In Memory of W.B. Yeats"

I could say *my hands are butterflies and you
are milkweed* but in truth I don't know
what milkweed is, or looks like: only that *milkweed*

is somehow lovelier than *gravy stain*—
though what I know of butterflies,
what they are and love, is what I learned once

at summer camp: when a Monarch lit upon
Annie's shirt that hour after evening mess.
We gathered on the pebbled trail outside the dining tent

while Annie stilled her thin body, almost not breathing,
any of us, as the copper hinges of its wings flexed
and the long black tongue unfurled itself to lick

gravy from Annie's shirt. Nothing moved
in that whole Wisconsin dusk except
the Monarch's tongue, curled and coy as an eyelash,

flicking on Annie's shirt, tasting our same brown supper.
We hadn't learned *proboscis*, we hadn't learned
that *gravy stain*, despite its assonance, its tonal flow,

owned some particular unloveliness. That hour, I flared
my hands back, fingers stretched, to balance my leaning-forward
toward the Monarch's tongue, our spiraled center. You,

hearing this now, could say *I don't think butterflies
have tongues.* They don't, of course, that's true. Yet
what I am trying to say is *yes, they do.*

Elegy: My Brother at 18

Cranked *Carpenters Gold* when he thought he was alone.
Put on *Who's Next* when he heard me come home.
Worked at the Jewel stocking shelves, but wouldn't cashier.
Said he "didn't need the hassle."
Played every sport, even golf; got stoned.

Kept his curtains from when he was five—called them
"the best curtains a boy could own."
Chased me wild eyed, and I guessed must have meant it
to miss when that Louisville Slugger got thrown
at my head: it tumbled past end-over-end
like a cyclone.

Pelted my window with rocks when he forgot his key.
Crashed his Camaro then walked all the way
From the E.R. home, stitched tight.
Came drunk, clamoring up, sat ass in the bathroom sink.
Leaned his head against the guy in the mirror and winked.

Let me ask him, "if you could be any animal, what would you pick?"
Furrowed his bandaged brow to think. Said
"A panda. Then everyone would love me." And that

is what I remember: mild skull-socket eyes
and the black black smile, born blind, rarely seen
in anything like a natural habitat.

ZOMBIE APOCALYPSE BEGINS TODAY

I know why this is happening:
why memory has called you back

from the coolness of earth,
with your bloody hunger and eyes full of rain.

You are slow, and no longer
the one that I loved.

Dear Heart, dear shambler, gather up
your self, your starveling intent.

In this new world, even the end
is not the end, the white light retreating.

I heard you say as you were leaving,
I will try not to come back.

I will try not to come back,
as if what happens next is ever up to you.

Circumstance in its orange cap
has drawn a bead on us, so we'll move on.

Bring repose and its rusty music,
what sticks to your sleeve as you amble by.

Bring night, bruising the sky.
Behind it, the night drags the morning.

Dear Heart, little stumbler, you've grown
strange in the straining light. Still,

you are mine, and you cannot help it.
This is our new world now,

still spinning, reborn from ash
into ashen. So we'll move on.

The headline tells the news,
but not the story: *APOCALYPSE*.

So much work, all this beginning.

My Brother's Body

My brother lost his body
bit by bit—a foot, a finger, a shin.

The doctors strapped it to a bed,
and the mouth screamed on its behalf:

Help! Help! With the eyes,
my brother spied me, standing

in the body of someone
who looked like his sister;

and the mouth said
Health! Health! but my

body had no way of sharing.
Stubborn, he set his body

to starving: it's a hard going.
One day I tricked it

into eating cake
by saying we were at a party.

The body likes to do what
everyone else is doing.

When he was done with it,
I could tell: every limb

he had left sighed, sank
and rose again softly, like smoke.

Like smoke: when he was done,
my brother had his body

set aflame. My body, always
dutiful, arranged it.

In the white room, roses, burning.
Then it was over. I took him home.

My Mother

Consider this: a can of soup.
My mother, shopping, lifts her hand
to the white shelf, thinking of days
she'll be too tired to cook, full days
of caring for her home, tending
her grown son; imagining
a warm meal and that it will keep.

She later lifts her white hand
again to a white shelf, listening
for her ailing son; in the pantry turning
the label forward so it can be read,
not thinking of habit, not thinking
before the cold comes everyone
living in this house will be dead

and today I eat the soup, imagining
vegetables greening in the yellow sun,
the swelling shoots, the impossible
machine coaxing each young pea
from its split velvet chest.

The Pear

Eating the pear that ripened on the windowsill
I think of my mother

saying to her fatherless children
at supper

*if you can't finish, or won't,
at least eat the meat*

which she learned as a fatherless
girl shivering with her mother:

but if there were time or world only
for one more bite of this

soft-spilling flesh, this gold
greening ripeness

I would eat
from the bottom of the pear

where gravity has pooled
the sugar.

MARLENA WAS A MERMAID

Poets on the Alien Planet

In the schools, if they have schools,
the young things curl over desks,
if they have desks, with their laser pens or sodio-
styluses or nanocrystal pencils colored like zoo animal
skins (if they have zoos), completing
worksheets to practice the names
of their moons, all seven.

One may be named for its burning;
one for its bluish cast; another for the way
it seems to wander in that far sky, its elliptical
orbit stretched by a mineral gravity.
One may be where they keep their angels,
or their weapons, or their dead;

or where their babies come from,
in stories told to take the place
of the cruel or ridiculous mechanics
of their species. There is always a smallest,
and a largest, and the moon most slip-shod,
disreputable, butt of their inscrutable
jokes, Pittsburgh of moons.

And the alien poets (for they must,
so moon-rich, have poets) likewise curve
their bodies (the curvable parts—if only their
however many moonward eyes) around
the odd implements of their odd craft,
which seem to them so ordinary,
so incapable of capturing anew

the particular beauty tonight of
Iominia, how it kisses the soft slope of Sirek6
with light (a phenomenon they all have seen
before, given the length of their solar orbit). Still,
they are compelled to try, because they are
in love, or lonely; or because

they are poets, and their word for *azure*
is strikingly similar to ours.

Homunculus

Sweetiepie, Monkey,
little genius
of despair.
I know you

are in there,
pulling levers
behind my dura,
that chintzy curtain.

That's you, rattling
at two round windows
sunk into
the bony wall;

you, flinging yourself
onto the flounced
grey bed. You practice
volition (those boring

offices) like a
creaky violin,
the same dumb scales
over and over.

When will you take
your drop of honey,
your dish of milk?
When will you

sweeten, sweeten?
You send your
susurrus down the
snakey canal:

I'll never, I'll never.
You are disturbing
the world's
smallest anvil.

Marlena was a mermaid

when she was a girl. Well, half-mermaid:
beguiling as her mermaid mother,
irises green and milky as beachglass,
ears curling like pink snails.

Now, she is a dental hygienist.
Molars and incisors form tiny reefs
for her instruments to swim around
like gobies: imagine
opening the mouth of a bear
and seeing a little dollhouse.
This is what it is like for her.
Sometimes when the children lie back
on the blue wave of the chair,
the tender kelp of their tongues
brings a homesickness almost like joy.
Marlena can't help but lick
her own tears when they come.

She is tired of being always
attached to some surface
like an appliance, her hair choking
on its own brown weight.

She thinks Mr. Eliot's poem must be
the saddest and most beautiful
in our oxygen language: a man
hears Marlena singing with her sisters
in their red summer wreaths and,
hearing their music, despairs.
Each time she reads this poem,
Marlena's heart tears a little:
Of course we sing for you!
she cries. At least the poem
ends well. Marlena bends

above a coral-edged mouth
and says *open, please.*

Snow White and the Huntsman

She called a huntsman, and said,
'Take the child away into the forest...
Kill her, and in this box bring me
her heart as a token.'

They gave me the child, and I took her gladly.
She was singing, no fear in her heart.

They gave me a jeweled box, a silver knife.
Imagine—to me, with my hunt-bloody hands.

We journeyed in soft snow. Her sigh,
the sound of a partridge wing on snow.

The night sky closed around us, a jeweled box.

Before that night, I had never turned from duty.
Why would I? It fed me, it made me.

I had taken from the world already so many
soft things, and she seemed like another.

But her song, sung to the dark trees, moved me—
like a shadow on the snow, I could not keep it.

Because I could not keep it, I would not take it.
Desperate, I prayed to whatever swayed the branches.

My answer, the white ring rolling in the black
branches: the soft, wide eye of a trapped hart.

I drew the silver knife. I filled the jeweled box.
The girl ran into the shivering trees

and the bleeding world swayed away from me.
Beneath the rolling stars I was charmed, changed.

Now: rabbits bare their snowy throats for me.
Even the wolves, whining, offer their softest selves.

This morning a white dove drove itself
onto the tip of my unmarked arrow,

and my heart closed around it.

The Way Home

Little by little,
they let sweetness back in:
a bite of seed-cake;
a thread of honey
dissolving in tea.

Some evenings Gretel visits,
brings apples for his children,
who sleep, eventually,
leaving their father with his
gold-haired sister,
heads bowed together,
alone in the flickering,
trading the secret
names they gave the strange dainties:
Pink Royals, Angel Tarts.
They remember jam
shining like church windows,
the fat flies' lullaby drone.

In her apron she
folds a finger bone.
In his pocket,
one white stone.

Mrs. Hood Confesses

I tossed her into the woods like a match
with its head struck. Blazey girl,
lalalaing with a basket

of day-old loaves and my smallest
chip-lipped pot for the butter.
Little GoBetween, I should have named her.

Yes, I admit to a hardness in me.
I saw only reproach in my mother's
big, big eyes, couldn't look

at them without shrinking.
So I sent my girl, my daughter,
my rosy little pork chop.

Tonight when they all burst in still slick
with wolf, I hardly believed the tale:
but when the woodsman swung his axe

in demonstration, the girl flickered back
with her white, pretty teeth.
I flushed, remembering

that I was the first to peel flesh
into light for her, pushing her
into the world wet and red. Yes,

I regret almost everything before this,
but not this. Look at her now: she shines
like a summer plum, blushing, taut

with juice. You can say it should have been me
that made the journey: the sun-freckled path,
the birch bones bending above her like a ribcage

as she went on, reliable as a clock.
True, things might have gone badly,
but here she is whole. Now my mother folds

inside her rosebudded bedclothes:
in the morning, I'll bake her a honey cake.
In the morning, if she lets me,

I'll wash my daughter at the hearth.
I'll brush her black, black hair
into sparks.

Pinocchio After 40

*Whilst he slept he thought that he saw the Blue Fairy,
smiling and beautiful... imagine his astonishment when
upon awakening he discovered that he was no longer a
wooden puppet, but that he had become instead a boy, like
all other boys.*

Blue,
are you there?

      (Crickets, the ghosts
      of crickets. Wind-creaking pines.)

Blue, I've seen things
with these knots that became eyes.
Was I a child when I clapped my hand
across my mouth
to stop the animal bray
rising in me?
             My kids:
we've heard it, Dad, you were stuck in a fish,
but they don't know. I wouldn't
want them to. Still
I say *whale,* they sigh,
          whatever.

Forgive me, Blue:
Sometimes I'd have them
made of wood, just to keep them,
      to catch a splinter
      and swell around it.

All this leaving:
my friend went first, the long-eared
cohort of my wilder days,
him dead on the street in his traces
and me crying in the gutter
like a fool.
My good father, gone too.
Even the days, like green needles
slipping through snow.

From that first moment of flesh

it's a softening,
       and I didn't expect it.

The world doesn't pull on me anymore.
I am tired, being made now
      of a thousand things.

You loosened the spark, became
the first thing I lost,
my last thought in the dark,
listening to the children rustle in their beds
like leaves.

Blue, I know
you hear me: answer.

Orpheus, Resigned

I sang beauty over and she stayed.
Isn't that most of
love?

We were happy, for a minute. Hoping
love alone can save
is a grave

mistake—death came, and then
the golden chance I blew.
I fell into

gloom, scorned all; lazed and gazed up, blue.
Now you mad women: you'd tear me up,
my song's such a drag? Fine.

I gave, now I'm undone.
In Hell I'll get what's mine.
Love is a grave I fell into.

Icarus Decides

Half my boyhood spent
dogging you around that maze.
My barrow of rocks
I pushed as if they
mattered to your grand
plan. I was your own
half man: even then
I could tell your brain
would dwell and dwell.

And when it all fell
apart, what'd I get?
Locked in. With you, the
architect of everything.
It was there I grew
incrementally
away, spiraling
from your stone-walled
center, and still stuck.

True, it wasn't all
bad: some nights we'd be
companionable, almost,
crouching around a
stuttering fire. We'd
spit-roast the seabirds'
plucked bodies; with smoke
we'd slacken the bees
into a stupor.

Now this: your latest
plot, strapped to my back.
Already you are a speck,
dissolving. For one
moment I test being
separate, nameless
and teeming as the sea.
Then I feel the day
flare around me and

I choose. How I fling
my body outward—
do you see? I am
a wild thing of your making.
Calling, I commend
myself to wing, to
sky, to finally
astonishing you.
I ascend.

Persephone of Maple Street

They were in the tangle
behind the garage with the weeds
and the neighbor's dogrun stink. But pretty,
peeking out like tiny hearts
of birds in the grass. So she plucked.
A little white thumb stuck up
from each stem in the berry's place.

In a palm cup she carried them
to where her husband was sweating.

Want some of these berries?
But he wouldn't take any,
got angry because of the heat,
or the berries, or the weeds.
Always there was work
no one wanted to do.

The boy nearby pretended
to be poisoned by berries
so everyone would laugh, but no one did.
She thought the boy was beautiful
as a bowl-eyed pony.
She should have named him Shadow
or Buttercup.

A whole summer in her mouth,
the berries.

She said *you know what this means?*
But the man did not say a thing.
So she answered herself:
Now I have to stay here.

Whatever You Call It Will Be Its Name

He gave me this task as if becoming
myself, into myself, were not enough:

that was how I saw it, at first.
I carried it like a stone too great to set down.

Then one day I began it, as if by accident:
animal, I said inside, to distinguish my hunger

from yesterday's hunger, which I came to call
fish. Then *bird*. Then beyond bird to *singbird*,

then *tik-sharoo, berrythroat*. After each word
that creature would come to me, leaping

into vision from what had been before
just a blur of what I called first *green*,

then *celedon, clover, myrtle, pear, longleaf,
riverwater-in-evening-sunflare* until

what I came to call *a voice* said, *maybe you should stop*.
But I had set that stone down hard,

and in time the gifted muscles of my naming
first trembled then flew with the lightness of it:

only after *leopard* did each crowd of black flecks
assume the shape of my fingertips. *O, praise,*

I name this: bigger than *need* or *want*
and in the end, that is the test of it.

Dear Mrs. Death:

There are problems at school again.
Often your daughter seems lost
in her own little world. Today,
when I asked her to stack the reading books,
she caused a calamitous nation
to rise and fall on the middlemost shelf
as she lined up books with their spines facing out.
When she writes at the board, each atom of chalk
trembles with the effort of clinging
to that blackness.

All of our classroom mice have ceased.
Her ponytail is somehow mighty.
What emanates from your fair daughter's
fingers, from the ends of her grey-gold hair,
is distracting to the other students.
Is this her usual state?

Mrs. Death, I'm sure you can see my concern.
On the playground Thursday a splendid bird
arose from the wood chips beneath the swings.
Was it a phoenix? A firebird?
This is not my area of expertise,
but I feel you may shed some light.
It was a glorious, shimmering thing:
each feather a subtle history; its votive eyes;
and I saw (we all did) the infinite
curve of its compassionate claws—

I must tell you we believe that your daughter was involved.
Has she ever done something like this?
I am sure, in the end, we all want what is best.
Mrs. Death, since that day
I cannot stop weeping.
Call me, please, to discuss.

Alan Shepard Is Created As God

Houston… you might recognize what I have in my hand as
the handle of the contingency sample return; it just so happens
to have a genuine six iron on the bottom of it.
—Apollo 14 Commander Alan Shepard,
preparing to hit golf balls on the moon

I was reborn into tiny millions.

Flickered at first, but then
I was Profound. I understand it now,
though not in a way I can profess to you.
The eons having passed.
My old blue home still hanging there,
a wild gratefulness in Me
at the sight of it.

As testament I reveal now a great secret:
They were Titleists, smuggled in the crook
where thigh meets body, one on each side.
The first I hit, nothing came of.
The second connected, and having
Gathered from Me some speck
carried it out spinning into the sea of dust.

Sweat, or my own cells—some Self repeated
—became life, dimple by dimple,
over long waves of time breaking,
slow tides frothed by the persistent sun.
Not like Me but wholly Me, and needy.
I answered by becoming.
Does it seem self-important to say

I am Apollo now? I am Shepard
and a new creation.
I am miles and miles and miles.
I look back on My time in flesh
as a history of angels,
earnest, forever
casting ourselves out.

Dear Atlas:

Of all the Titans, I would say that you're
my fave. Your picture's on my closet door.

Others see muscles like Missouri; I
see the blue interstate of you, a place
I can drive myself into like a root,
send shoots down into your busy marrow,

that bloody factory. I would be
the inbetween of you, Atlas, the way
you are the inbetween of Heaven, Earth:
bipolar, feet in the sweaty ocean

and shoulders prickled by the needling stars.
I love how the sky doesn't murder us,
how even daffodils, with their big dumb
faces and skinny necks, will get a chance.

I understand it all: your igneous
skin; your melancholia, the tide
that brings boats in. With me, you're not alone.
I feel the way you keep us on the lip

of earth beneath the lip of sky. Dear Atlas,
the others don't see what I do.

I have a book of maps and call it You.

MIGRATORY

Migratory

Late September. Leaves scutter, then the first call
of the Canada geese—the necessary noise
of fall, the squall of creatures who would rather be
elsewhere. At the sound I gaze up: gauge their southness
against sunset, watch as two dozen or so point the arrow

of their array to a more temperate place
of memory. The flock passes over so low I count
the black webs of feet pressed back, the speckles of down
on rounded breasts; and the stretched throats,
for one moment, hush: only then I hear

the under-sound that must be
always there, a steady *whoosh-shwoosh*
woosh-shwoosh of drafting wingbeat, each stroke pushing
downward on the cushioned air, treading
sky. It is a strange recycling:

how nature can borrow a sound—say,
the deepwater revelation of my then-unborn son's heart
learning its rhythm, a sound I last heard on sonogram
some twenty-one autumns ago—and let it drift
now from the blushed sky, borne earthward
by the dark press of wings.

Baking Ghazal

Today, I practice making kolacky. Outside, the turning leaves.
Poring over my mother's recipes, I cried while turning leaves.

I fold two points of each square to the middle: small, crossed hands.
Colors of apricot, berry, darken inside, like turning leaves.

Like my mother, I make kolacky, and I want to get it right.
Waste, a bitter taste: the sugar-scorched underside that burning leaves.

Some I cut too large, ungainly. Some crack; some open, leaking jam.
The best: wee swaddlings on the nursery-pan. Comes wide yearning, leaves.

I haven't burned a single one. Soon holidays, I'll double the batch.
Like my mother, I pencil notes, margin-side: what learning leaves.

Like a mother on school mornings smiling doorside who, turning, grieves,
I practice making kolacky. Outside, the turning leaves.

Squash Blossom

To the party I wore your necklace

which I have never worn before:
I didn't think that I could manage it,
that I could be so ornamental and specific;
but today I plan my wardrobe with white
shirt like a sheet to lay

its jeweled body upon: spreading
its shining fingers of beaten silver,
the dark-veined knuckles of stone
colored like desert sky in just evening,
dry summer thrumming.

Everyone loves your necklace,
putting on their glasses
to examine it more closely, turning
the slender trumpets to peer in
at each narrow shadow.

To those who remark I say the same thing:
Thank you, it was my mother's
it was my mother's.

Walking home in blue dusk,
I want to show you the necklace:
how it settles on my chest, its bearable weight,
so I turn my throat to the sky I imagine
as you, say *look at this lovely heaviness*
which deserves more than its box

and suddenly I want to know how turquoise
is mined, I want to see the river of rock supple
beneath the earth, I want to bring water
to the ones who freed it from stasis,
polished it, brought it to the light.

The Burn

The burn pouts its pink lips out
and behind them grinds its tiny teeth.
The burn is a new way to be in my kitchen,
saying *look how red* the poppy
on this dishcloth, its opening petals.

The burn puffs like a narrow fish
the tidal day has trapped on my arm.
The burn first draws itself in, then flings
its imaginary screech. Like everything,
it responds mostly from beneath.

The burn will linger for weeks:
for weeks my finger will trace it back
to the bubbling dish I pulled from the oven,
I'll hear the young cousins' wild running
on the Easter lawn, the hiss of my arm
pressed to the rack, the sister-in-law at my back

sighing in sharply: *ooohh, I've done that—*
shall I call everyone in? Are we ready?

Love Poem

Steal
from summer
one sun wild
blackberry

so tender
it tears   bleeds
onto your
open

palm
your soft tongue
it is yes
sweet it is just

enough

The Fiery Skipper

Could be wings are an affliction,/a different kind of tyranny.
—Li-Young Lee

A fiery skipper—lepidopteran,
small as a cent and colored
summer gold and bronze,

alights in the wide margin
of the book lying open
on the grass in bright sun

and first casts a scale from its wing
onto the page, where the scale becomes
the saffron dot of an invisible *i*;

and next closes its deepest ochre,
sorrel, sepia, between wings it holds
like a knife, edge toward sun;

and next regards its narrow silhouette,
which falls forward from
the hair's-width feet and runs

beneath the skipper's form
to lie plain before it on the page,
to demonstrate its shadow-body

as human, without wings: abdomen, waist,
chest and shoulders, a round
head that nods once

beneath twin antennae,
the several legs merging in shadow
to just two. The skipper lingers there,

motionless, for what may seem to a butterfly
a week of time, all in morning.
Suddenly it seizes the air:

assaults the sky flaring above
the waving tips of grass
and swings free,

like the pilot

who ejects, wild-eyed, from the burning
body of his plane to find himself
alive, hurtling in space:

and can tell at once by tenderness
that every vessel in his face,
now bruising grey and golden, has burst.

King of the Death Match

There was a boy who loved wrestling so much it became a mania. Not Olympic wrestling but professional wrestling, hard core, King of the Death Match and Battle Royale. The boy devoted himself to his pursuit until it became the subject of all conversation, the focus of all activity, the metaphor by which he explained everything else. His mother never liked professional wrestling but she loved the boy, and so she admired his authentic high-laced boots, black patent leather; she learned turnbuckle and apron, supplex and hammerlock. She knew that Sick Nick Mondo's real name was Matt Burns, and understood why this was funny. This is how it went for half the boy's lifetime, every day, in his leisure and schoolwork, the friends he chose and the clothes he wore, absolutely every day until the day it stopped. He gave it up entirely. It had never made him happy, he said, he'd only thought for eight years he'd known what happiness was, but felt now that life offered so much more. He got an electric guitar. Things disappeared from his room and were replaced with other things; the boy grew his hair and they had long conversations about what Led Zep's stairway really was, and why it could never be bought. Then one afternoon while the boy was at school and the mother was cleaning their home, something winked at her from a dark corner of the spare closet. She reached far in, pulling very hard until the object slid forth in a rush. A slick, black-soled boot. She burst into tears, huge wracking sobs; then she heard the back door open, and she stopped.

Mustang

How much sugar will you take?
Dear marshbrown boy,
dear specklebrown egg, dear
browndown drake. My porridge, my cake.

You say, *what do you think?* and I tell you. We talk
for an hour, maybe more: moths tick-tick
their chalk against the glass. Each neat star
is a slip-stitch of white in the sky's dark fabric.

You slide back your chair. Upstairs,
you tune the Fender Mustang we let you get.
Now I stop considering the Infinite, grateful
about so much milk in your coffee, the sugar,

since you'd had no supper, in spite of me
offering to rustle you up some eggs. Listen:
e e e, a a a, d d d, g g g.
The song that says you are happy, or about to be.

How I Know My Son Will Keep His Job

This was a mistake, he says, slumping
into the passenger seat after that first 8-hour shift.

We are in the loading lane at the Jewel
and the good citizens push their metal carts and heft
groceries into vans and trunks, white plastic or brown paper
bags with the stems of bananas jutting out; they swing
24-packs of pop up from the bottom rack
and cross back and forth between the lines on the pavement.

The blue Jewel polo tagged with his name
clings to his body and wants a wash.
Well you need to stick it out, I say finally, *at least
for the time they took to train you.*

Two shifts go by, maybe three, same scene. Then
one day a woman with her plaid jacket open to the wind
shoves her empty cart to clang against another
in a vacant parking spot, where both carts drift a bit,
uncertainly, as if either one might make a wobbly
break for it. *I fucking hate that* says Jake, glaring
not at me but at the woman, who has turned away.
Double-strays. I hate that.

I say, *oh, double-strays. Is that what they call it?*
That's what I call it, he says, and I know.

Nineteen

This poem
is about my boy, in the kitchen, reading to me a poem.
About my boy, nineteen, reading to me a poem from a book he has chosen
casually from my stack of books, and he flips it open and begins to read.

My boy is nineteen, and the poem on the page that falls open
is called Sixteen, and he reads it aloud to me, he is allowing me.
It is a poem about a boy. The boy in the poem, the boy in the kitchen:
they become the same, one a little grown past, the other approaching.

Grinning, my boy finishes, beautiful. And in the kitchen every thing
is so: the yellow wood, the scarlet poppies on the porcelain cups
in the cupboard behind his head, the brown shock of his head. Everything
he has just read to me, he has been to me, my boy, a poem in the kitchen.

I am praising his reading, his aloudness of Sixteen, and aloud my boy asks:
It's about him, right? meaning the poet, and the poet is a man I know,
not a young man, and my boy thinks that Sixteen is about this man. I say,
no, it is about his son, his boy. *Not him as a boy?* my boy says, and I see

the wonder of this poem: it makes a boy forget he is not a man;
he reads the poem and it becomes about him, and he has become the poem.
He is part boy, part poem—the boy thinking then that he must be
an old man, or that the poet must be a boy. A poem.

This poem
is about a man—no, a boy, my boy, and we are there in the kitchen,
the scarlet shock of nineteen and the porcelain cups. I hold my boy
in the way he allows me, and I fall open, holding him.

Anniversary

There is something strange on our mailbox,
arabesqued atop the box's black hump

like a circus performer on an elephant's back.
All the same on our Saturday street except that.

We're just on our way out. You say *What is that thing?*
and I tell you *It's a cookie.* Sweet and square

as a handkerchief. It balances perfectly
near the catch that keeps the black mouth of the mailbox

from falling open. We've lived here, cookie-free,
for twenty years. Through the day's errands

we speculate about who could have left it there:
a neighbor kid? An Adventist? Our postman, James?

I suggest *squirrel* and you question a motive.
You ask *what kind?* as if I know every cookie. Is it a gift,

a message? A souvenir? Now we are finished, we have
the dry cleaning and everything, a light rain begins.

On our street we pass the mail truck with its blind, blue
eagle, and you pretend to be James calling out to us: *Hey*

didja get my cookie? Now home, we've both gone goofy.
The thing is still where we left it, though in the rain

it has softened, swelled, eased itself down to assume
the rippled curve of the mailbox, ready to dissolve

and smear when James brings the bills. *I'll be right back*
as I grab a kitchen towel and you call after me *thanks.*

Today, you're at work and I'm here. Then I find it
in the grown-out boxwood by the barbecue grill:

a cookie, resting flat and pale on the dark needles
like an icon held aloft by the faithfuls' hundred hands.

With my phone, I snap a picture: what do we get
here that we ever understand? Wind swings

the door shut; I'm in socks on the driveway.
I send you the picture, though I know you'll believe me.

Oblation

One sun-stunned drop
of blood this August night,
half the town wilting on damp grass,
the singers swaying to what we already know
about the heart: *the roots of love*
grow all around

Now the swans drag their silver wake
on the pond in waning light.
We'd shared paper-wrapped sandwiches,
spilled wine on a child's flowered blanket, for a long while
I held Rosie while she slept. The sky
bruised through its changes.

So take it, the blood meal, your ruby
belly arcing out in flight to a secret
shadow you know. I felt wingbreath, that sweet disturbance,
in the fine hair on my arm before the pinprick,
I didn't mind it. Clouds color and swell,
mirrored in water. *Goodnight,*

goodnight call the singers. The townspeople
rise and stretch, reach toward the halogen lights
you are mad for. Tonight, if enough of you—crazy from music,
so much light and blood—take our bodies into
your bodies, lifting out over water: I will
yes. Say *yes.* I will say *yes.*

My Dog, Long Dead, as a Tiger

It follows an undetermined apocalypse.

Our new friends are having trouble
with their tiger. He's not himself.
He seems sad, and in his sadness

he has become violent. I agree
to speak with the tiger, which is led in by a rope
at his neck, swinging his kingsnake tail.

He is barely unpouncing. He is coil
and roil, gaze and glare. Suddenly, I am aware
that in him flows the reincarnate spirit

of my 20-years-gone dachshund. He only wants
to be called by his old, true name, which I know,
so I say it: *Spaulding, Spaulding, it's me.*

His eyes have two pleadings: an inward,
that his own teeth and claws not tear me up,
and an outward, that I should continue to speak

his true name, *Spaulding*, the name of my dead
dog; not *Sampson*, which was his tiger name.
In time we grow quiet, recline on the smoldering

sofa in the ruined room, enjoying each other's
company, the sunset giving its thin broth of light,
his orange head on my chest like a boulder.

I am so busy burying my hands and face
in the deep plush between his ears
that I forget to ask how the world ended.

Tonight, Everyone Is in Love

Tonight, everyone is in love.
Gaze at the face
of the spilling moon
and tell me this is not so.

Tonight,
a child is in love with an arm,
a boy is in love with a car,
a woman's in love with a photo

of a man, of course, in love.
Old stories, true, but
tonight, wet with the fiery moon,
again we can love them.

One hundred striped spiders
are in love
with places in my house
I am afraid to go.

Tonight, a bride
is in love with a groom, a groom
is in love with a bride, a guest
is in love with

the groom's pierced
ear, which is all she knows of him,
and with the way his black jacket moves
to show he is crying.

The cake on the table is
in love
with the knife my mother uses
to bless it.

Tonight, everyone is in love.
Look at the night's blazing buckle of moon
and try telling
the desperate stars otherwise.

A girl is in love with a book tonight,
and the book is in love
with the swans' necks of her sweet fingers
along its cracked spine.

Even the ram, its head inclined,
is in love with the thicket
where he waits in
white moonlight burning

for Abraham,
whom he loves.
Tonight, under the spilling moon,
I confess to you:

everyone is in love.

THE EYE

Part

of the yellow-eyed bird
on the fence.

My brown hair he knows
from the strands in the nest
of his just-hatchedhood.
It's you!
says the yolk-yellow eye, *how*
I've missed you, and the humped
sheen of sun on his black chest
flutters, heart about to burst.

And of the red-velvet mites,
when their tiny

selves streak like comets
in a whorled heaven.
No matter how careful my fingertip.
I am their sky falling and falling.
Bright and horrible!
They forgive all morning
in frantic little circles.

Oh green world, pretty day fading,
help me be a part,
part of, never from.

Of the white day and its exploding.
Its quiet, its birchbark

girlhood. I want to slip into, I always
have wanted. The whispering,
the whimpering, the way the leaves.
The aim of my true blue,
the object of my mad crush—
it's you, of course, I say to the bird.
It's you, it's you.

To Galileo, Grinding Lenses

I want to believe
the story of the well:

every day I would travel
down in a bucket
if it were true that,
looking up, I'd see
day-veiled stars.

From clay, look now:
The root-stubbled deepness

inverts, becomes something
vaulted, piercing. The light is shut
out, the curls of cloud separate,
the blue slip of skin
dissolves. Finally

the sky, that lick-thin
membrane, opens

to spill some hidden constellation—
what beats, constant,
just beneath the surface:
the bleat
always waiting

in a lamb's
limber throat.

One Could Have a Cape Made Entirely of Buttons

And it would deflect bullets.
And it would shimmer like the scales
of a rainbow fish leaping up.
Each button would be the subject
of an historical treatise
written after years
of torturous research.

One from a doll's dress, no, her eye.
One from the shoulder of a shroud—
but no, it is not what you think.
One button would depict the life
of an obscure and lesser saint,
scrimshawed
on the bone of a famous whale.

This is not a thing one would ride
roughshod over. Not a coarse thing
discussed over back fences.
Believe me, thousands of the faithful
hoi-polloi would have
gathered here, fevered,
had I remembered to alert

the proper authorities. True,
the hands that sewed each button on
first rocked kings in their crude cradles.
True, it can predict the weather
but it's not very accurate.
Stricken with fear,
its enemies recoil.

And once again, I mention here
that it can deflect bullets.
Or would, of course. I should say would.
If such a thing, but... well. You know.
Just be advised that you have been
advised. You all might as well
drop those guns.

The Eye

I admire the eye, which inverts
the inverse, therefore righting.

It dilates. It sleeps. It peeps
through a pinhole at the horizon,

which is false, and which retreats
in response to the eye's advances.

Its humors: like glass, like water.
The whipblack lashes.

Open, even behind its skin.
I want to be aperture, to let in.

How to Build a Bird

Use a feather for the engine. No:
a feather for the idea of engine,
each barb pointing at the hollow
calamus, its memory of flight. There.

Wind a hair around your fingertip
to make a kind of armature. Here
is the thrumming you'll need, the pulse that pools
your blood to tenderness, its red prayer.

Borrow from other things that you have built:
the brown frog's holy regard for the pond
he sets ringing, his plash like a temple bell.
Borrow the bell's regard for shiver and air.

What else have you built? Learn from this; glean.
If you're thinking *yellow,* say *canary, finch.*
Use a scent from memory for the song—
or for the keening, or wingflash, or flare.

Bone: use twig, pearl, ivory, reed. What matters
is the binding, the needlework. Think of
the cactus spreading out its sharp music
and sew. Save the glint for the bird's bright stare.

Save each trimming. Save the feather, too.
Cup your hands. Press your mouth to what
you have built, all you have tried to build,
to the grail of your hands, brimming. There.

Poem to Franz Wright

We love people

who agree with us
about the world.

You write
> *If they stabbed me to death on the day I was born, it*
> *would have been an act of mercy.*

Wah, you cried, we all did. Who would call it forethought?
No one would

do as you say—not father, doctor. It wouldn't be
the nurse that pulled the small knit hat

onto your squalling head
or onto mine, the same. Even blue:

Franz, they told *my* first mother I was a boy
before whisking me away for good!

What do we know about mercy, really?
We only mean ourselves.

And what do we know about that?

Machine, Horse, Rider

Once the season has started, or is about to start,
if you're northbound on 53, and the day
is fair and you're in the far right lane, glance
over the guardrail to the practice track:

you may get a glimpse of the sprayer trucks
misting the surface to keep down dust,
or the harrow combing ridges into dirt
as true and sweet as a macaroon's.

It's best when the horses are out. You can't
see the practice track from the grandstand
or backstretch; not from the slant-roof stable sheds
or the dorms, or the paddock or parade park;

you can't even see it from 53 South.
Only in that diesel-drab half-mile between
Industrial Road and the ramp to Route 14
might you just catch them, just

running—doesn't matter what the horse is named,
or the jockey; what the wager is, or purse;
or that the track looks cobbled up from curves
cut from three better tracks; and the silks

don't matter since there are no silks, no why;
just machine, horse, rider, rush, flash: see
all those hoof-hurled divots,
their small, brilliant urgency.

The EOSINT M280 Laser Sintering Machine is ideal for precision fabrication of medical implants.

The techie presses
into my palm
a titanium

vertebra,
unflawed, stippled
with pores created

by the process:
a bright beam burns
layer and layer

of sifted metal
dust, which fuses;
then the formed piece

rises from dust
whole, a new shape
to puzzle into

the body's tangled
geometry.
The vertebra

is soundless, almost
weightless, it has
symmetry on two

axes. I like to bring it
to my eye while I
tilt up the shade

of my desk lamp:
see the sprung light try
to fight its way

through those dark
channels, where in
another body

we'd find, like white
threads of a bean
shoot, bone.

Red Study

Left hook lands and
fighter's tooth

frees itself
from the ruined architecture
of the mouth

rushes out
above taut canvas
flings one   shining

        cardinal flash
        against a winter
        treeline

of blur-stained
faces, stunned

Loss of the Thing

I pushed my heavy mower, blades whirring,
up a rain-runneled patch of lawn, until
the strain buckled the handle, pitching me

toward the whir: in spite of which I still
gripped—hard!—the dead-man's switch. Now I could see
the nut was missing from the bolt securing

the handle to the body of the mower.
Imperceptibly, row after row,
the motor's vibrations had coaxed it up

the spiral staircase of the bolt's threads,
like a square creature, shyly taking dropped
crumbs of bread. It had followed where they led

and, breaching the bolt's end, it tumbled down
into the deep mystery of the spring lawn.

The loss of the thing tossed me, made me pitch,
white-knuckling the mower's dead-man's switch.

Dust

Through rain, watch two workmen in frayed coveralls
cross the bridge, and as they walk

see their footprints seem to rise from the rain glaze,
like distant ringed villages seen from a great height.

The footprints form two rows, as if those villages
are strung on either side of a river, and there is the great height,

and mist that dissolves to reveal them, village
after village, and the moss-colored river as it flows

between. (This is just before night, when the sky
lets slip down its flinty jacket.)

Now set to laying your own steps between theirs—follow
as a small sister might, at a little distance,

as if the river imagined between them is your path.
Advance, then slow, and look back

to see that you're leaving no footprints at all:
the space between the workmen's footprints

remains pale as a blank receipt. Consider,
for a single stopped moment, whether somehow

you may be dead. One workman turns his head,
then the other, to catch sight of you; they gaze

from above the grayed respirator masks shifting
loose at their necks, and now you see the fine dust

caked in their eyebrows, sifting from their coveralls
onto the walk, brushed down by the whisk

of the rain; it is dust that marks their way,
which fell on them at their work and now falls

away, forming shapes like ringed villages
along a wide river flowing forward, into mist.

To Galileo in Autumn, When the Atmosphere Cools to Stillness

Now I drag my telescope onto the lawn

and point its massive eye up:
amid crickets, the clammy grass, returning twice to the house
to click off a lamp—it takes forever to sight onto
Jupiter's steady prink of fire,

to focus, turning the screw until the juice
of light runs clear enough to see the surface:
striped with orange, the spot
like blood in a child's half-opened mouth,
bright, narcotic poppy.

I pick out Ganymede, Io, Callisto, Europa:

your proof, strung
like a rosary's preliminary pearls.
You called the Milky Way *nothing else
but a mass of innumerable stars*
as if that were not enough:

our spiraling heliocentricity,
the blessed, mathematical relief of it.

The past is alloy, gigantic

There was a motorcycle—cobalt blue
plastic, about 16 inches high, white handlebars.
My son rode it, a mad abandon, clacking
in our basement, down the sidewalk, no engine
but the legs he used to have, attached
to the body he used to have, small and milk-stuffed.
Where are you going? I'd ask, folding laundry.
I'm going to see my old mommy. This was the '90s:
what did we have then? Chlorofluorocarbons,
Apple IIs. It was hip-hop's Golden Age.
He called it "mugger-cycle." His riding was a sea.
This was a long time ago, to him and me.

The past is alloy, gigantic. Nothing goes away.
Everything is somewhere, my old mother
used to say. *Your windbreaker did not grow legs
and walk off by itself.* I went back to the park:
there it was, pockets stuffed with seedpods
I'd gathered, a finite universe. Bee-velvet,
the twitching rabbit I'd stalked: that was that day.
I already carried the cells that would be my son.
Petroleum waited beneath that Earth to become
the plastic; before that, as algae—leafless, Paleozoic—
it drank sun, that simple ardor. It could never
not be. Like boy, body, jacket, riding, sea.

Apple

The tight eye
of the apple
squeezed shut:

here, my
finger finds it

where the wrinkled
sepals cluster closed,
where once

blew the white blossom.

If I cut
across the apple's wide

horizon
inside I will find
the star

unseen,
corecut star, star-

flower
memory, petal bones,
in white, dark

seeds.

About the Author

Jan Bottiglieri's poems have appeared in a variety of journals and anthologies including *Harpur Palate, Court Green, Bellevue Literary Review, Rattle* and *Sunrise From Blue Thunder*. Her chapbook *Where Gravity Pools the Sugar* was published in 2013. She is a freelance writer and editor living in suburban Chicago, and serves as managing editor for the literary annual *RHINO*. Visit her website at *janbottiglieri.com*.

Other Recent Titles from Mayapple Press:

Kita Shantiris, *What Snakes Want*, 2015
>Paper, 74pp, $15.95 plus s&h
>ISBN 978-936419-51-7

Devon Moore, *Apology from a Girl Who Is Told She Is Going to Hell*, 2015
>Paper, 84pp, $15.95 plus s&h
>ISBN 978-1-936419-54-8

Sara Kay Rupnik, *Women Longing to Fly*, 2015
>Paper, 102pp, $15.95 plus s&h
>ISBN 978-1-936419-50-0

Jeannine Hall Gailey, *The Robot Scientist's Daughter*, 2015
>Paper, 84pp, $15.95 plus s&h
>ISBN 978-936419-42-5

Jessica Goodfellow, *Mendeleev's Mandala*, 2015
>Paper, 106pp, $15.95 plus s&h
>ISBN 978-936419-49-4

Sarah Carson, *Buick City*, 2015
>Paper, 68pp, $14.95 plus s&h
>ISBN 978-936419-48-7

Carlo Matos, *The Secret Correspondence of Loon and Fiasco*, 2014
>Paper, 110pp, $16.95 plus s&h
>ISBN 978-1-936419-46-3

Chris Green, *Resumé*, 2014
>Paper, 72pp, $15.95 plus s&h
>ISBN 978-1-936419-44-9

Paul Nemser, *Tales of the Tetragrammaton*, 2014
>Paper, 34pp, $12.95 plus s&h
>ISBN 978-1-936419-43-2

Catherine Anderson, *Woman with a Gambling Mania*, 2014
>Paper, 72pp, $15.95 plus s&h
>ISBN 978-1-936419-41-8

Victoria Fish, *A Brief Moment of Weightlessness*, 2014
>Paper, 132pp, $16.95 plus s&h
>ISBN 978-1-936419-40-1

Susana H. Case, *4 Rms w Vu*, 2014
>Paper, 72pp, $15.95 plus s&h
>ISBN 978-1-936419-39-5

For a complete catalog of Mayapple Press publications, please visit our website at *www.mayapplepress.com*. Books can be ordered direct from our website with secure on-line payment using PayPal, or by mail (check or money order). Or order through your local bookseller.